NATIONAL GEOGRAPHIC

NATIONAL GEOGRAPHIC

THE ANGRY BIRDS™ MOVIE

Red's Big Adventure

CHRISTY ULLRICH BARCUS
FOREWORD BY MIKAEL HED

NATIONAL GEOGRAPHIC

Washington, D.C.

Published by National Geographic Partners, LLC, 1145 17th Street NW, Washington, DC 20036

Library of Congress Cataloging-in-Publication Data

Names: Barcus, Christy Ullrich, author.
Title: National geographic The angry birds movie : Red's big adventure / Christy Ullrich Barcus ; foreword by Mikael Hed.
Other titles: Angry birds movie
Description: Washington, D.C. : National Geographic, 2016.
Identifiers: LCCN 2015040596I ISBN 9781426216848 (paperback) I ISBN 9781426326097 (hardcover)
Subjects: LCSH: Angry birds movie (Motion picture) I Nature in motion pictures. I Nature--Humor. I BISAC: HUMOR / General. I PERFORMING ARTS / Film & Video / General. I NATURE / General.
Classification: LCC PN1997.2.A54 .B38 2016 I DDC 791.43/72--dc23
LC record available at http://lccn.loc.gov/2015040596

Since 1888, the National Geographic Society has funded more than 2,000 research, exploration, and preservation projects around the world. National Geographic Partners distributes a portion of the funds it receives from your purchase to National Geographic Society to support programs including the conservation of animals and their habitats.

National Geographic Partners, LLC
1145 17th Street NW
Washington, DC 20036-4688 USA

Become a member of National Geographic and activate your benefits today at natgeo.com/jointoday.

For information about special discounts for bulk purchases, please contact National Geographic Books Special Sales: ngspecsales@ngs.org

For rights or permissions inquiries, please contact National Geographic Books Subsidiary Rights: ngbookrights@ngs.org

Interior design: Nicole Lazarus

Printed in the United States of America
16/QGT-QGLM/2

CONTENTS

FOREWORD 6

LEVEL 1   BIRD ISLAND   8

LEVEL 2   BIRD VILLAGE   46

LEVEL 3   THE SEARCH FOR MIGHTY EAGLE   84

LEVEL 4   BEYOND THE ISLAND   122

ACKNOWLEDGMENTS 158

ILLUSTRATIONS CREDITS 159

FOREWORD

As you'll see in *The Angry Birds Movie,* Bird Island is a pretty cool place to live. It has great weather, warm seas, and plenty of quirky feathered fauna living in (almost) perfect harmony. In fact, it's not so unlike many islands across the globe.

For instance, did you know that nearly half of the bird species found on the Galápagos Islands are unique to their environment? That sounds like Bird Island! What's more, Piggy Island, the land of pigs like Leonard and Ross, isn't the only place that's ruled over by naughty piggies . . . Big Major Cay in the Bahamas has its very own Pig Beach, where wild pigs call the shots!

You'll find out about all this with the help of the guys at National Geographic, who have been special friends to Red and his pals since 2012. So sit back in your deck chair, sip on some pineapple juice, and discover everything there is to know about island life!

Mikael Hed
Chairman
Rovio Animation

Explore the island with Red and the Angry Birds

Who says mornings have to be good?

Away from the flock, Red lives alone in a seaside hut on the edge of town.

AT HOME ON BIRD ISLAND

Far out in the middle of the ocean lies lush and isolated Bird Island. This tropical hideaway is home to unique birds living peaceful, happy lives.

BIRDS IN PARADISE

Abundant forests cover Bird Island's steep mountains, and streaming waterfalls flow down its rocky cliffs, emptying into turquoise waters. Anything a bird could want, from worms and fruit to shopping and meditation, can be found within the island's shores. The birds who call this island home are one lucky flock.

WELCOME TO THE FLOCK

Warm sunshine and cool island breezes create a thriving environment for the bustling community of birds living on the island. Busy birds flurry down Main Street as they cheerily go about their day, chirping with friends and tending to their nests. Some birds, like speedy Chuck, dash in for breakfast at Early Bird Worms. Expectant moms attend Matilda's prenatal yoga class before returning home to the nest. One bird, however, isn't all that happy.

THE ORIGINAL ANGRY BIRD

Meet Red: He's gained a reputation as a fed-up, flustered, and down-right angry bird. Red built his sea-side hut far away from the other birds on the outskirts of town. As hard as he tries, Red can't seem to fit in. Even when he has the best of intentions, his temper flares up or his actions end in disaster. He struggles to find his place in the world.

Red takes comfort in reading tales of Mighty Eagle, the legend-ary warrior of Bird Island. It's said that Mighty Eagle has always val-iantly protected the village and its precious eggs. Red hopes he can achieve something as spectacular as Mighty Eagle's accomplishments one day.

BIRD ISLAND'S GREATEST HERO!

Red admires Mighty Eagle, a legendary bird on the island known for his courage and strength.

ZING NEW ADVENTURES of MIGHTY EAGLE

ON ISLAND TIME

Thinking of islands conjures up images of sun, sand, and surf. But islands can range from lush tropical forests to windy ice-covered expanses. The formation of each island (any body of land surrounded by water) varies depending upon its underlying geological history.

GET THE DRIFT

Two of the major types of islands are continental and oceanic (also known as volcanic) islands. Earth's relatively thin crust lies atop its much thicker mantle, a hot semisolid rock layer about 1,800 miles (2,900 km) thick. The crust and upper mantle, called tectonic plates, collide and shift over time, forming continental islands, so named because they were once connected to a continent. Many of these islands, such as Greenland and Madagascar, broke away from the mainland millions of years ago but still lie on the under-water continental shelf.

Other continental islands came about at the end of ice ages, when glaciers melted and sea levels rose, creating low-lying areas away from the main continents, such as the divide between the British Isles and mainland Europe. Oceanic islands like Hawaii were created by undersea volcanic eruptions, often in the interior of tectonic plates.

Paradise comes in many
forms, from hot lava
flows on the Big Island of
Hawaii (opposite) to lush
green cliffs in Ireland.

FIRE AND ICE

From humid jungles to polar deserts, island conditions vary wildly around the world. Oceanic islands form from volcanic eruptions, creating rich landscapes like the Hawaiian Islands archipelago, which spans 1,500 miles (2,400 km) in the North Pacific. Archipelagos, or groups of many islands close together, form in oceans and sometimes in rivers and lakes.

CHAIN REACTION

The Hawaiian Islands chain formed from an eruption over a hot spot in the middle of a tectonic plate, which caused magma to rise upward and erupt on the seafloor. Active volcanoes today continually change the landscape of the Big Island, with its jungles and lava flows. However, volcanic fires on the other islands—such as "the garden island," Kauai, the oldest major island in the chain—have cooled as tectonic forces have moved them off the hot spot.

Islands with little precipitation are considered desert islands—and they're not always hot. At the top of the world, Ellesmere Island, a polar desert, is a land of ice and snow. Yet the island, the northernmost in the Canadian Arctic archipelago, hosts a surprising diversity of animals. Arctic wolves and hares blend into the barren winter landscape. In the summer, when temperatures rise, polar bears hunt seals and walruses in open waters.

The sheer fluted cliffs of Kauai's Na Pali Coast provide a stark contrast to the Arctic ice fields of Canada's Ellesmere Island (opposite).

WORLD HOT SPOTS

Trade winds, ocean currents, and weather patterns influence island climates in unique ways. In the Galápagos Islands, Pacific currents collide at the Equator, creating fertile habitats. UNESCO recognizes this volcanic archipelago, with its distinct climate, as a World Heritage site.

Anybird up for a race?

BIRD BLISS

Off the southeast coast of Africa, isolated Madagascar's coastal rain forests and mangroves are habitats for native tropical birds, such as the brightly colored Madagascar pygmy kingfisher and the rufous-headed ground-roller.

Some island homes are distinct for people, too, like the tiny British outpost of Tristan da Cunha, arguably the most remote inhabited island on Earth. Halfway between Argentina and South Africa in the South Atlantic, windy weather dictates the pace of life on the 38-square-mile (98 sq km) volcanic island. Yellow-nosed albatrosses make nests from tussock grass, and spiky-haired northern rockhopper penguins, which locals call pinnamin, gather in rookeries along the coast. Just over 250 human residents, most of them potato farmers and lobster fishers, live there full-time.

A colony of rockhopper penguins
scales an island in the South Atlantic.
Opposite: A pelican perches in a
mangrove tree in the Galápagos.

EXTREME ISLANDS

BIRD ISLAND HOSTS INCREDIBLE CHARACTERS ON AMAZING ADVENTURES. ISLANDS IN THE REAL WORLD ALSO HARBOR INCREDIBLE SPECIES LIVING NOTEWORTHY LIVES IN A VARIETY OF ECOSYSTEMS.

MADAGASCAR, AFRICA

The island nation of Madagascar, located off the southeast coast of Africa, possesses remarkable biodiversity. Ninety percent of the plant and mammal species on this island cannot be found anywhere else on Earth. Unique lemur species make up nearly half of the island's mammals, and 40 percent of the world's chameleon species live on Madagascar. However, human developments pose threats to wildlife. The International Union for Conservation of Nature (IUCN) recently declared lemurs the most threatened mammal group in the world.

GALÁPAGOS ISLANDS, ECUADOR, SOUTH AMERICA

In 1835, upon first seeing the giant tortoises of the Galápagos Islands, Charles Darwin noted that they appeared like "inhabitants of some other planet." An ecosystem of stunning diversity, the Galápagos lie some 600 miles (965 km) off the Ecuadorian coast. Thousands of species thrive on the islands, including the marine iguana, the Galápagos penguin, and the blue-footed booby. Nearly half of the island's birds and insects—and 90 percent of its reptiles—live nowhere else on Earth.

Changes to Madagascar's landscape, such as this patchwork of rice fields, impact wild-life habitat today.

Pigs love eggs-treme islands!

GREENLAND, NORTH AMERICA

More than three times the size of Texas, Greenland is the largest island on Earth, covering more than 840,000 square miles (2.175 million sq km) in the North Atlantic. Its glaciers and fjords enticed the Vikings from Scandinavia, who established settlements on the edge of the island in the tenth century A.D. Today, about 85 percent of the island's population is Inuit. Greenland's massive ice sheet, second only to Antarctica's, holds almost one-tenth of the world's freshwater.

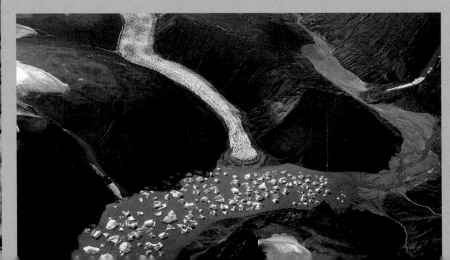

RED
ANGRY AND MISUNDERSTOOD

In the happy-go-lucky community on Bird Island, Red's a real loner. The nonstop cheery attitude of the other birds really ruffles his feathers. He lives a solitary life in a seaside hut away from the rest of the flock.

Infamous around town for his temper, Red's eruptive nature and sarcastic attitude only mask his real discomfort about feeling like an outcast. Although Red usually wants to do the right thing, his temper gets in the way. His attitude makes it difficult for him to form friendships, like the time he meets Chuck and Bomb in his court-appointed anger management class.

But after a herd of piggy outsiders arrives on Bird Island, Red's natural distrust gives him important insights that the rest of the flock lacks, and may determine the very future of the island. Red is fiercely protective of the island's most precious resource, its eggs (the next generation!). Although a reluctant leader, he may finally prove to the rest of the birds—and himself—his true worth.

WIND AND WAVES

Island life hinges on temperature and weather, from cold and windy to hot and humid. North America's Great Lakes system drains into the most extensive estuary on Earth, the Gulf of St. Lawrence. In the gulf lies Canada's Prince Edward Island, which receives a healthy spray of sea salt, wind, and fog.

SEA BREEZES

Known as the Garden of the Gulf, Prince Edward Island harbors mussels and lobsters, along with huge colonies of breeding birds, such as double-crested cormorants, great blue herons, and piping plovers. Native species thrive in its salt marshes and rose-colored dune system. Its lowland forest and red-clay paths give rise to hardwood trees. The island's tourism is driven by Lucy Maud Montgomery's *Anne of Green Gables,* a book about an orphan heroine who relishes the wild beauty of her island home.

More than 8,500 miles (13,500 km) away to the southwest, Palau, an archipelago of more than 500 islands in Micronesia, dots the western Pacific. Coral reefs, atolls, caves, and mangrove swamps teem with marine life. Golden jellyfish, giant clams, and reef fish dart among its vast coral reefs. Hawksbill sea turtles find plenty of food in the island's coral crevices, where they use their pointy hawk-like beaks to tear away sponges.

Turquoise waters wind through Palau. Opposite: Wind-rippled dunes stretch across Canada's Prince Edward Island

Any eggs down there?

ISLAND EVOLUTION

One hundred eighty years ago, a remote 19-island archipelago surprised naturalist Charles Darwin with its revelations. Lying in seclusion far off the Ecuadorian coast and spread across 50,000 square miles (130,000 sq km) of the Pacific Ocean, the Galápagos Islands act as a natural laboratory of biodiversity. Here Darwin formed his revolutionary insights over the course of just five weeks, later fueling his theories about natural selection and adaptive radiation, when one species branches out from a single ancestor to become many.

BLOODTHIRSTY SPECIES

Darwin witnessed how 13 species of finches exploited ecological niches on the various isolated islands, pushing birds to adapt in different ways. The birds selected different diets, some pursuing seeds, others insects, flowers, and leaves. One species, the sharp-beaked ground-finch, locally called the vampire finch, even developed a thirst for seabird blood.

Oceans away, the island nation of Madagascar also illuminates species evolution in isolation. The satanic leaf-tailed gecko, one of several species of leaf-tailed geckos found only on Madagascar and nearby islands, blends effortlessly into leaf litter piles, thwarting birds of prey, as the carnivore hunts at night for its next meal, which may include insects, small rodents, or even a reptile.

Keep walkin', partner!

ALBATROSSES

Graceful and elegant, an albatross glides easily across the sea. Its impressive wingspan, the largest of any flying bird, allows it to ride the wind great distances without expending much energy. Yellow stripes mark its heavy bill, and specially adapted nostrils secrete excess salt from seawater. These iconic birds breed on oceanic islands and then quickly head back to sea.

BIRDS-OF-PARADISE

Stunning plumage and bizarre mating rituals reflect the wild tropics where birds-of-paradise thrive. Flying across a narrow band of diverse forest in New Guinea, Indonesia, and Australia that's largely devoid of predators, these standout birds aren't afraid to show off their flamboyant feathers. Spectacular head plumes, crests, beards, and long tail streamers distinguish the 39 species. One of the most stunning may be the greater bird-of-paradise, with its yellow-and-green head and elegant tail.

The volcanic environment of Hawaii's Big Island creates lush forests.

Vampire finches on the Galápagos Islands **drink the blood** of seabirds by **pecking at their backs.**

I'd stroll down that Hawaiian path!

Cowrie shells and **hawksbill sea turtle shells** have been **used as currency** on different islands.

Bermuda's **pink-sand beaches** get their rosy hue from **tiny marine organisms** called red foraminifera, which **grow on coral ledges.**

ISLAND ADAPTERS

Animals specialize and evolve in different ways to fit the unique features of their island homes. In the sunny lake waters on the island of Palau, two marine creatures have formed an unlikely friendship with mutual benefit. An algae-like creature, zooxanthella, converts sunlight into sugar, which it shares with its symbiotic host, the golden jellyfish. Millions of jellyfish follow the arc of the sun a half mile (0.8 km) across Palau's aptly named Jellyfish Lake, avoiding the dark shadows near the lake edge, where their anemone predators live. Luckily for snorkelers, these jellyfish are essentially sting free to humans.

BALANCING ACT

Madagascar's largest carnivore, the fossa, preys on the island's lemurs, rodents, and reptiles. Though it may look like a cat, the 20-pound (9 kg), long-tailed animal is a close relative of the mongoose. The predator helps keep the ecosystem in balance, but as the dry, deciduous tropical forest where it lives is reduced in size, its numbers have dwindled. Scientists estimate that there are fewer than 3,000 fossa left in the wild.

Incoming!

Golden jellyfish follow the sun's rays in a lake in Palau. Opposite: A fossa prowls a Madagascar forest.

LIVING ON THE EDGE

DESPITE THEIR INCREDIBLE ADAPTIONS TO ISLAND LIFE, THESE ANIMALS FACE UNCERTAIN FUTURES.

SUMATRAN TIGERS

Found on the Indonesian island of Sumatra, only an estimated 500 Sumatran tigers remain in the wild. A shrinking habitat and conflict with humans threaten the critically endangered subspecies, which at up to 300 pounds (135 kg) is the smallest type of tiger. With comparatively narrow bodies, large manes, and webbed paws, Sumatran tigers stalk deer and wild boar across dense tropical jungles and into peat swamps, where they even swim after prey.

A Sumatran tiger navigates island waters.

I'll help protect you!

GALÁPAGOS TORTOISES

A 500-pound (225 kg) giant, the Galápagos tortoise holds the record as the world's largest living species of tortoise. Naturalist Charles Darwin even rode on a tortoise's back when he visited the Galápagos Islands. Tortoises eat prickly pear cacti, fruits, flowers, and grasses. Some finches on the islands have developed a mutually beneficial relationship with the reptile, feasting on the ticks found in its neck folds. Today the Galápagos tortoise is considered a vulnerable species.

KOMODO DRAGONS

One of the fiercest animals alive, the Komodo dragon is the world's largest living lizard. Growing up to ten feet (3 m) and weighing 200 pounds (90 kg), this monitor lizard basks in the sun, lays eggs, and scavenges across the volcanic Indonesian archipelago. It reaches speeds of 12 miles an hour (19 km/h), its mouth dripping with venomous saliva as it ambushes its prey and tears its flesh. Its dinosaur ancestor lived 200 million years ago, but today fewer than 5,000 of the vulnerable species remain.

CHUCK
FAST AND FURIOUS

Overflowing with energy, Chuck zips around Bird Island like a bird on a mission. Fast-talking, quick-moving Chuck likes to make friends. He's a performer, and even when his moves end in disaster, Chuck never slows down. Like a peregrine falcon, he's the fastest in the flock, and he's always ready to strike. No challenge is too big or small for competitive Chuck. He's happiest when he's showing off!

His need to please sometimes works against him, though, like when he meets Red. In his typical hyperactive manner, Chuck runs through a series of moves to impress his new buddy and the rest of the flock. But Red can't be bothered with Chuck's dizzying energy.

After the pigs' arrival, Red needs a friend he can depend on more than ever, both for himself and to preserve the future of the flock. An unforgettable journey lies ahead: Will Red open up to Chuck and accept his friendship in a quest to protect the eggs?

SHIFTING SANDS

Standing along the coastline looking out to sea, many have contemplated life's mysteries. "My soul is full of longing / For the secret of the sea," the poet Henry Wadsworth Longfellow wrote. "And the heart of the great ocean / Sends a thrilling pulse through me."

FLOCKING TO THE BEACH

Shaped by the forces of Earth, moon, air, and water, beaches are constantly changing form. Beaches are created by ocean waves that bring loose sand or other sediments that accumulate over time. Waves crash against a beach an estimated 6,000 times a day.

Wind and water transform the coastal environment, and the regular ebb and flow of the tides shift a beach's profile. Dunes help protect shorelines from erosion by absorbing storm waves and protecting what lies farther inland. Although few plants can grow in sandy environments, dune grasses, such as sea oats, help anchor sand in place. Dynamic dune systems create rich habitats for plants, animals, and marine life.

People enjoy living by the coast, too. About half of the world's human population lives in urban areas, and the majority of them live within 60 miles (100 km) of the sea.

Seagulls (opposite), sand dunes, and sunsets converge at the beach.

WATERS COLLIDE

Don't want this to collide with the floor!

Beyond the ocean's immediate shoreline, coastal regions encompass rich ecosystems called estuaries, where fresh river water and salty ocean water meet. Floodplains, mangrove forests, marshes, tidal flats, bays, and barrier islands are all part of productive estuarine environments. Estuaries act as filters, removing pollutants from rivers and streams, to create cleaner, healthier waters that eventually drain into the ocean.

NATURAL BARRIERS

A continental shelf underlying estuaries forms barrier islands, which run parallel to the coast and protect land and nearby waters from ocean pummeling. Estuaries can form behind groups of barrier islands, like North Carolina's Outer Banks. They are connected to the ocean by inlets. Wind, waves, and wild beauty converge at the Outer Banks, which extends for nearly 300 miles (480 km). Towering dunes also serve as powerful barriers on the Outer Banks. Nearby Jockey's Ridge, the tallest active dune system in the eastern United States, provides a windy playground for hang gliders, kite enthusiasts, and a pair of famous fliers. The Wright brothers used the windy conditions to their advantage for their epic first flight in 1903.

Oregon Inlet in North Carolina's Outer Banks connects ocean and inland waters.

SEASHELL STANDOUTS

ALONG THE BEACH, SEASHELLS REVEAL THE FASCINATING LIVES OF TINY MARINE CREATURES.

SAND DOLLARS

The sand dollar is a disk-shaped invertebrate marine animal. When it dies and sunlight bleaches it white, it resembles a coin. Living sand dollars range in color from forest green to violet. They use tiny hairs, called cilia, to dig into the seafloor and scour for algae and crustacean larvae. A cousin of the sea urchin, sand dollars have radial symmetry, often displaying five-point radial star markings. They resist strong currents by using their spines to burrow into muddy ocean bottoms in the Atlantic, the Pacific, and the Gulf of Mexico.

Natural treasures of the surf, sand dollars look like flat coins.

CONCHS

Beachcombers and foodies both prize the conch. This large sea snail's conical shell flares open, with spiky bumps forming near the tip of its spire. The snail's meat is used in conch chowder, conch ceviche, and more. Found throughout the Caribbean Sea, the Gulf of Mexico, and Brazil, conchs lay eggs in shallow-water reefs and sea-grass meadows. Yet overharvesting is a threat, especially to queen conchs, which may reach one foot (0.3 m) in length and weigh up to five pounds (2.25 kg).

COCKLESHELLS

"With silver bells and cockleshells," the nursery rhyme "Mary, Mary, Quite Contrary" famously goes, highlighting the heart-shaped clam found in shallow tidal salt water and estuaries around the world. More than 200 species of cockleshells filter water and feed on plankton. They range in size, with diameters from 0.4 inch to 6 inches (1–15 cm). Peach-colored on the inside, the connected twin shells of cockles display ridges, or ribs, that radiate outward.

SANDS OF TIME

The next time you kick off your flip-flops and dig your toes into the sand, think about this: Is it smooth or rough? The way sand feels on your feet reveals important clues about its formation and the mixture of minerals, rocks, and soil particles that make up sand.

SANDY CRUSH

Most beaches in the United States contain ground-up granite flowing from rivers to the ocean. Smooth, white powdery sand comes from quartz, a common type of mineral found in rocks. Siesta Key Beach near Sarasota, Florida, contains some of the world's finest and softest beach sand, composed mostly of quartz. Cobble and pebble beaches are near the edges of eroding, rocky cliffs.

Pieces of different rock crystals, shells, coral, and lava create sand, too. The black-sand beaches of Hawaii owe their distinctive coloration to lava flowing from active volcanic eruptions. As the lava hardens, waves crash into it and create tiny pieces of volcanic glass, which accumulate into a black-sand beach. Plants easily take root in this mineral-rich environment.

Pink-sand beaches form as surf crushes red shells and coral reefs over time. Soft blush-colored sand, like on Bermuda's Elbow Beach, is the stunning result.

Black-sand volcanic beaches in Maui contrast with older beaches composed of quartz and other minerals (opposite).

I'll just dip one toe in . . .

45

LEVEL 2 BIRD VILLAGE

Visit Main Street and Bird Court

Normally concealed beneath Judge Peckinpah's cloak, it's Cyrus who really gives the judge a leg up in Bird Court. Looks matter on the island, but appearances can be deceiving.

WHEELS OF JUSTICE

In Bird Village, Main Street is a flurry of activity. Parents take baby birds for walks, run errands, and stop to chat. Many gather in the amphitheater, where Judge Peckinpah delivers his judicial verdicts. A statue of the venerable Mighty Eagle stands watch over the court, its powerful wing pointed toward the sky.

RED'S DAY OF RECKONING

In a series of unfortunate events, Red manages to squash a cake instead of delivering it safely to a young bird's birthday party. After Red ruins the party, the young bird's parents bring him to face the court's justice. An outcast on Bird Island, Red alone must defend himself before the court and Judge Peckinpah.

THE LONG WING OF THE LAW

Despite Red's honest testimony and explanation of the many circumstances behind the botched caked delivery, the judge delivers a much dreaded sentence: anger management class. It's the worst-case scenario for Red—someone's going to make him talk about his feelings! And to top it off, the class is taught by Matilda, who will even force him to do crafts and yoga!

Red doesn't embrace yoga instructor Matilda's anger-free philosophy, but Chuck is eager to show off his moves.

FRIENDS OR FOES?

In anger management class, Red meets fast-talking and faster-moving Chuck, as well as Bomb, who's fun enough until he gets too excited and explodes. There's also Terence, the biggest of all the island birds, and one of the least communicative; he hardly makes a sound, except for an occasional grunt.

Although Chuck and Bomb are friendly, Red's not in the mood to make friends. Chuck's attempts to show off and mimic Matilda's yoga poses don't impress Red either. But these two birds might be critical to Red's future—and the fate of Bird Island.

BIRDS OF A FEATHER

Like the Angry Birds on Bird Island, birds in nature often live in large colonies on islands. Naturally social creatures, birds benefit tremendously from mutual cooperation, which helps them survive as they hunt and mob potential predators as a group (think Alfred Hitchcock's movie *The Birds*).

FLOCK TOGETHER

Flamingos have some of the largest colonies, from Africa to South America. The fantastically pink, social birds concentrate in huge numbers, with more than a million of them gathering together in lagoons and near the edges of shallow, often saline, lakes to suck up algae and shrimp.

In the spring and summer, Atlantic puffins breed in colonies along rocky coasts. The so-called clowns of the sea are noted for their beaks, which turn orange during breeding season. They build nests on cliffs, where each mother lays a single egg, and both parents take turns incubating it. Puffins return years later to the same island of their birth to raise their own chicks.

Some birds, such as pelicans, travel together. They fly in lines of V-formation to take advantage of collective airflow and help conserve energy. Professional cyclists apply the same aerodynamic tactic when they race in teams during competitions like the Tour de France.

Cotton candy-colored flamingos flock
together. Opposite: Puffins' beaks
turn orange during mating season.

LOVE IN THE WILD

Love can be wild in the bird community. With nearly 10,000 species of birds on Earth, these relationships can look and sound very different, depending on who's involved. Some species, like albatrosses, are family guys that form monogamous pairs, while others, like birds-of-paradise, show off their suggestive intentions through elaborate dance moves. Then there are the romantics—bowerbirds, for example—that rely on the timeless gift of flowers, decorating the entrances to their bowers with petals and fruit, among other items.

THE RIGHT MOVES

Perhaps none is more theatrical than the superb bird-of-paradise on the island of New Guinea. With its black cape of feathers and shock of turquoise streaking across its chest, a male puts on a flamenco-worthy performance to entice females to mate. As it vocalizes a snapping sound, a cape of feathers fans above its body and it hops left, right, and back again. Repeat!

Male emperor penguins romance potential female mates during harsh winters with offerings of the rocks native to their Antarctic home. In this bird colony, penguins make nests with a mix of tiny pebbles and large stones, creating piles a few inches (centimeters) high, sometimes with a piece of driftwood added for flair. The male also incubates a single egg for up to two months.

Emperor penguins embrace family life. Opposite: In New Guinea, a male superb bird-of-paradise raises his cape to attract a female.

NEST IS BEST

Nests, like birds, come in all shapes and sizes. The primary focus of a nest is to create life for the next generation. And when it comes to baby birds, the main concern is safety. During springtime, birds search for a suitable nesting site protected from weather and dangerous predators like snakes and foxes. As in real estate, location is key. In the classic children's book *Make Way for Ducklings,* a pair of mallard ducks flies all around Boston searching for just the right place to make their nest so Mrs. Mallard can lay her eight eggs.

That's one eggs-cellent nest!

BREAK ON THROUGH

From mud to sticks, birds' nests take many forms. Some species construct camouflaged circular nests in trees, while others burrow holes into cliffs along riverbanks. Others, like woodpeckers and northern flickers, excavate wood by drilling into trees to create nest cavities.

After baby birds hatch from their eggs, parents ready their young chicks for independence, and it's usually time to fly away. Most nests are abandoned by both chicks and parents, making bird parents true empty nesters. But before they leave the nest, juvenile birds have a lot to contend with—in North America, songbird nest predation rates range from 25 to 80 percent.

Excavating a nest cavity, a northern flicker drills through a tree. Opposite: A mother mallard duck keeps her eggs warm.

HOME SWEET HOME

BIRDS ARE SOME OF NATURE'S MOST MASTERFUL ENGINEERS, CONSTRUCTING NESTS FROM GRASSES, BRANCHES, AND FLOWERS.

WONDERFUL WEAVER

A natural drive to weave fuels the weaver finch. With a loop here, a tuck there, and the twist of a knot, a male weaver engineers a well-crafted nest pouch at the end of a branch. It takes years of practice for the birds to learn how to make the structures. The roofed, woven chambers vary in style depending on the species. Many African species use grass or palm fronds as they weave their ball-shaped nests.

BOWER THE BUILDER

Male bowerbirds are nature's interior designers. They build elaborately crafted vertical structures, or bowers, and have an eye for order and detail, showing off for potential mates by building spectacular courtship bowers that allow passage through them, along with decorative stages out in front. On the island of New Guinea, the Vogelkop bowerbird decorates the front of its bower with artful piles of orchid flowers, beetle shells, acorns, fruit, and colorful leaves. Instead of a flat platform, its bower is a hut-like structure, with mosses added in front to create an inviting green lawn at the entrance.

In Kenya's Masai Mara National Reserve, a pair of vitelline masked weavers knit their nests.

Nobody's getting into these nests!

REGAL EAGLE

The national symbol of America, the majestic bald eagle inspires a sense of freedom as it soars. Its nests also inspire with their sheer size, some weighing a whopping 2,000 pounds (900 kg). Ranging across North America, from Alaska and Canada down to Mexico, bald eagles often reuse their woody nests, adding new branches and sticks each year. They prefer tall trees in remote areas near rivers, lakes, and coastlines, in places such as Yellowstone National Park, Wyoming; the Chesapeake Bay; Alaska; and Florida.

MATILDA
SERENE AND ACCEPTING

A reformed Angry Bird, Matilda now channels a Zen-like demeanor. She focuses on enjoying the sunny climate of Bird Island, with its warm beaches, fresh air, and rolling waves. She loves gardening and meditating, and she strives to live sustainably, even growing her own herbs, which she brews into a calming tea.

Matilda tries her best to avoid conflict without resorting to old angry habits. She leads the island's Infinity Acceptance Group, otherwise known as anger management class. Through yoga and deep breathing, she tries to model serene behavior. She wants her students—including Red, Chuck, Terence, and Bomb—to mimic her techniques and practice thinking through their feelings in a state of calm, without reacting in anger.

But no matter how many yoga poses she forms, or how many cups of herbal tea she drinks, old feelings of frustration and stress still linger inside of Matilda. More than anything, the thought of anyone threatening the island's precious eggs stirs up those feelings. Will Matilda's deep breathing pay off when it counts the most?

EAT LIKE A BIRD

When a person "eats like a bird," it's implied that they're eating very little. However, the average bird actually eats more "like a pig," consuming the equivalent of a quarter of its body weight every day. From earthworms and nectar to beeswax and fish, birds consume a variety of foods.

KNIFE, SPOON, AND BEAK?

The shape of a bird's bill, or beak, hints at what's on its dinner menu. The beak is a bird's main utensil, and it takes on a variety of forms. They may be tweezer shaped (for picking up insects), strainer style (for filtering invertebrates from water), nutcracker style (for opening nutshells), probing (for sucking nectar from flowers), spear-like (for stabbing fish), or hooked (for biting prey and tearing flesh). Sometimes a bird's name, like frogmouth, says it all.

Insectivores like bluebirds love to feast on mealworms, small insects, and berries. These songbirds, which help control insect populations, nest in tree cavities, or nest boxes that people provide.

Herons fillet fish with their long, strong beaks. They wade by rivers and ponds, quietly scanning the water as they wait to snap up their next meal.

Quite a mouthful you've got there.

A gray heron
snaps up dinner.
Opposite: An
eastern bluebird
catches a worm.

FEEDING FRENZY

Like a Swiss Army knife, a bird's beak has many uses—it's a utensil, weapon, sensory organ, and signal all in one. Beaks play an important role in nest construction, but their top purpose is usually gathering food. Foraging techniques include grazing, chiseling, probing, aerial maneuvering, and plunge-diving.

SUGAR FIX

Hummingbirds drink nectar from flowers through their straw-like bills. The tiny, colorful birds hover in the air, get a fix of sugary nectar, and then dart away to the next flower, which they pollinate. Hummingbirds need to eat almost constantly to fuel their extremely high metabolism and maintain a 105°F (41°C) daytime temperature. Only at night do they slow down; their temperature drops as they rest for the next busy day.

Noisy and aggressive, blue jays eat everything. These omnivores use their straight, powerful bills to devour insects, fruit, and frogs. With their hard bills, blue jays crack open shells for an acorn reward and raid other birds' nests for eggs. They also like to stash nuts and seeds away for later, but they sometimes do not return, leaving behind food that will grow into bushes and trees, spreading across the forest.

The search for food never stops: A ruby-throated hummingbird sips nectar. Opposite: A blue jay visits a bird feeder.

A feathered frenzy of activity surrounds a pod of pelicans.

Hummingbirds are the only birds that can fly backward.

Poison dart frogs contain lethal amounts of poison from eating tropical plants. Their brilliant coloration broadcasts danger to predators.

Male northern cardinals appear to kiss females as they feed them, all part of the bonding process.

CAN'T TOUCH THIS

Just like the Angry Birds defending their priceless eggs from marauding pigs, in our world, competition between animals often leads to a conflict. Animals develop defensive strategies and predatory skills to outsmart each other in the constant quest for survival in the wild.

PRICKLY PERSONALITIES

Boxing matches unfold outside the ring in Australia, where kangaroos sometimes duke it out in the streets. Males punch and kick as they compete for dominance and female attention.

In tropical oceans, a slow-moving fish defends itself with one of the world's deadliest poisons. The puffer fish (also called the blowfish) gulps enough water to inflate to three times its normal size. When it's blown up like a balloon, it's hard for a predator to wrap its mouth around the fish—some even have spines that stick out. If a predator does manage a mouthful, it probably won't come back for seconds, as puffer fish contain the deadly tetrodotoxin poison, which is powerful enough to kill most potential predators. Although toxic to humans, incredibly, the puffer fish is considered a delicacy in Japan, where licensed chefs are allowed to prepare it by extracting the nonpoisonous parts to eat. Bon appétit!

Two young eastern gray kangaroos in Canberra, Australia, aren't afraid of a little pushback. Opposite: A puffer fish's spiky appearance puts potential predators on high alert.

IN THE MOOD FOR FAST FOOD

Is this how you do it?

Predators must remain poised for their next attack. On the African savanna, even the world's fastest land mammal doesn't always get to eat its catch. With a body built for speed, the cheetah can reach speeds of more than 60 miles an hour (95 km/h) in just a few seconds and take down swift-moving prey like the Thomson's gazelle. However, its not-so-friendly neighbors—lions, leopards, and hyenas—often move in and steal its kill, causing the cheetah to lose out on its hard-earned catch to other animals. Its adaptive solution? Eat fast!

WATCH YOUR BACK!

Feared and admired, the northern goshawk is considered one of the fiercest birds of prey. Its fighting spirit has influenced warriors like ruthless leader Attila the Hun, who wore an image of a goshawk on his helmet. The goshawk maneuvers easily through forests in North America, Europe, and Asia. It hunts by ambushing its prey, gripping it, and tearing it apart with its talons.

A northern goshawk pauses atop a spruce tree with its latest catch, a Eurasian jay. Opposite: A cheetah races to take down a springbok.

ANGER MANAGEMENT IN THE WILD

THE ANGRY BIRDS AREN'T AFRAID TO STAND UP TO THE PIGS AND PROTECT THEIR EGGS. THESE SPECIES IN THE WILD ARE ALSO FIERCE FIGHTERS.

HONEY BADGERS

Don't be fooled by the honey badger's size—though it tops out at just 30 pounds (14 kg), this small mammal is a tenacious killer, able to bring down a crocodile or defend its food from a lion. Found in southern Africa, the Middle East, and India, this relative of the weasel family uses its keen sense of smell to hunt scorpions and puff adders. Its favorite meal, however, comes from raiding beehives and devouring the nutritious bee broods inside.

A honey badger in Yemen sniffs the air, searching for dinner.

MUTE SWANS

Outfitted with luxuriant white plumage, the mute swan gracefully glides across the water. Yet this seemingly elegant bird has a nasty streak. Fiercely territorial, it aggressively pecks with its bill, fights with its powerful wings, and sometimes even drowns its victims. Mute swans are among the world's heaviest flying birds, with wingspans up to 7.5 feet (2.3 m). Native to Europe and Asia, they are considered invasive species in North America.

PEACOCK MANTIS SHRIMP

This crustacean, ranging across the western Pacific and the Indian Ocean, looks a little different than you might expect. The peacock mantis shrimp looks like a praying mantis, but it's actually more closely related to lobsters and crabs. And it's a marine strongman, using its powerful club-shaped forelegs to take down prey. Prowling along the seafloor, it waits for the right moment, and then it kicks through the shells of unsuspecting snails and crabs.

JUDGE PECKINPAH AND CYRUS

POMP AND CIRCUMSTANCE

Some birds, such as Judge Peckinpah, just like the sound of their own chirp. Perched atop his sneezy sidekick, Cyrus, the judge presides over Bird Court's amphitheater. Due to Cyrus's allergic reaction to the lining of the judge's robe, muffled sneezes periodically punctuate court proceedings.

Given the happiness found throughout the Bird Island community, few cases actually come before Judge Peckinpah. But no matter how tame the infraction, the judge dutifully puffs up his feathered chest as he stands high and delivers his verdict with gusto. He enjoys his power over the flock.

But Judge Peckinpah may not be the best judge of character after all. When the pigs arrive, the judge, eager to maintain his influence and command of the court, cozies up to the pigs. Is the judge losing sight of what's really right and wrong—and will he be overruled?

BIRD BRAINS

The word "birdbrain" takes on a whole new meaning when you consider the corvid family. Corvids include ravens, crows, jays, and rooks. Their proven ability to solve puzzles, create tools, and make rational decisions shows how big a bird brain really can be.

SOLVING THE PUZZLE

Crows, ravens, and jays are social animals. They appear to understand the intentions of other birds and include that in their decision-making. In the South Pacific islands, the New Caledonian crow is a master carpenter, creating tools using branches and leaves—like a twiggy tool to reach into a crevice and retrieve a worm (see page 80)—and even refining them over time. The crow shares its techniques with others, too.

Macaws are also social birds. These colorful members of the parrot family mate for life. They identify their territory and each other through vocalizations. In captivity, macaws imitate human speech.

Life's a balancing act for this macaw. Opposite: Searching for a snack, a raven pries open a snowmobile's storage compartment in Yellowstone National Park, Wyoming.

BIRDSONG DUETS

It's said that imitation is the sincerest form of flattery. And birds are no exception. Several species mimic other species, meaning they copy another species' song, adding it to their song and making it their own. This musical mash-up increases a bird's repertoire, and it may even increase the song pirate's desirability.

Who said I couldn't carry a tune?

NAME THAT TUNE

Birds also build social bonds by making music together. Hundreds of species of birds, including wrens, sing duets with each other, strengthening their pair bonds.

The northern mockingbird is famous for mimicking the songs of others. Its scientific name, *Mimus polyglottos*, means "the many-tongued mimic." Common in the southern United States, from Florida to Texas, these birds learn hundreds of song fragments throughout their lives. They repeat each song at least three times. The bird is featured in the title of Harper Lee's novel *To Kill a Mockingbird*, where it represents the idea of innocence.

Parrots also learn by imitation, and they even vocalize and imitate human speech. By mirroring each other, parrots may strengthen their social bonds. The birds are able to render low notes that more closely approximate human sounds, unlike the high notes from smaller birds.

Mirror images, a pair of red-lored Amazon parrots face off. Opposite: A northern mockingbird sings a song from its perch in a tree.

WORLD'S SMARTEST BIRDS

FROM LAND TO SEA, BIRDS FIGURE OUT HOW TO SOLVE PROBLEMS IN MANY ENVIRONMENTS.

KEAS

As it soars among the mountains of New Zealand's South Island, the kea lets out a loud, long cry of *keeeaaa!* A curved beak and shock of orange under each wing distinguishes the large green alpine parrot. Intelligent and curious, keas are infamous for stealing food from hikers and taking shiny objects like car keys. They can also solve puzzles by pushing and pulling a series of objects to receive a tasty reward.

CROWS

Infamous crop raiders, crows are known as calculating and clever birds. These opportunistic omnivores form close-knit family groups, stealing and hiding food in the ground and in tree crevices. Yet crows can have a softer side, too, as an eight-year-old girl in Seattle, Washington, discovered. After sharing her lunch with the crows at her school bus stop, the birds surprised the girl one day. They started bringing her tiny shiny gifts, including beads, pieces of glass, and even a pearl-colored heart.

Psh, I'm no birdbrain!

RAVENS

In legend and literature, the raven symbolizes life and death. Brainy, and even playful at times, the large scavenger can solve complex problems through a series of actions. In a famous experiment, scientists dangled meat from a string tied to a tree branch to test a raven's intelligence. Without relying on trial and error, the raven made the correct logical connections on the first try, using its feet to pull up the string in sections, hold them with its claw, and repeat the sequence until raising the meaty reward.

Intelligent and social birds, ravens are known for their problem-solving abilities.

ALEX THE PARROT

Alex the Parrot is known as a pioneer in the world of bird intelligence. The famous African gray parrot worked in a lab for three decades with research psychologist Irene Pepperberg, who wanted to explore the intelligence and abilities of African gray parrots beyond mimicry.

ONE SMART BIRD

In the wild, these parrots inhabit African rain forests, but many are sold in the pet trade. Alex was purchased from a pet shop in Chicago, Illinois, in 1977, when he was about one year old.

Pepperberg wanted to understand Alex's cognitive and communicative abilities in comparison to other animals. Over time, she recorded that Alex knew the English words for more than a hundred different objects, actions, and colors. He could count sets of objects up to six and seemed to understand the concept of zero. He was also learning to sound out letters, and his favorite toys were key chains, cardboard boxes, and corks.

Alex demonstrated the ability to make connections in novel ways during his lessons. He surpassed bird benchmarks of language use. He even coached fellow lab birds Wart and Griffin as they worked with the scientific team. After Alex passed away at age 31 in 2007, the other parrots carried on his legacy.

A-parrot-ly, he's pretty smart!

Perhaps the most
famous gray parrot
in the world, Alex the
parrot demonstrated
incredible reading

LEVEL 3

THE SEARCH FOR MIGHTY EAGLE

Take an unforgettable journey up Eagle Mountain

Life on Bird Island heats up with the arrival of the pigs, led by Leonard.

MYSTERIOUS VISITORS

The days breeze by on Bird Island, until a mysterious wooden ship appears on the horizon. With its green flag flying, the ship comes closer to shore as curious birds flock together at the beach, busily chattering about what the foreign object could be. Bird Island has never had visitors before!

MEET THE PIGS

After the ship makes a rough landing, a portly green creature shuffles down a ramp and takes his first steps onto the island. With his smooth, featherless skin, protruding snout, and curlicue tail, this animal isn't like anything the birds have seen before. He introduces himself as Leonard, the spokesman for the pigs. He says they come in peace from a place called Piggy Island as he offers gifts to the birds as a token from their king.

THE WELCOMING COMMITTEE

The birds haven't heard of "pigs" before, or really anything beyond their home on Bird Island. The trusting birds heartily welcome Leonard and his crew, and they are delighted to show their new friends around. Led by Judge Peckinpah, the birds light up tiki torches, play chirpy music, and make a scrumptious banquet dinner for the pigs. The birds also give them a tour around the village, showcasing their most valuable possessions: their eggs.

HOLDING OUT FOR A HERO

But Red thinks the pigs are up to something—and it isn't good. Fearing for the safety of the island's most beloved treasure, Red decides to seek out the help of heroic Mighty Eagle. But without the ability to fly to Eagle Mountain himself, Red realizes he can't do it alone and decides to form a team. Along with his new friends Chuck and Bomb, Red sets out on an epic adventure, navigating the island's marshy swamps and sheer mountain cliffs in an attempt to find Mighty Eagle before it's too late.

At the top of Eagle Mountain, the trio finds the fabled Lake of Wisdom, the legendary source of Mighty Eagle's knowledge. But it turns out that Mighty Eagle may not be quite the hero they expected him to be.

Red worries about completing the team's journey as Chuck and Bomb make a pit stop at the Lake of Wisdom.

GO TELL IT ON THE MOUNTAIN

Every mountain tells a story. "Climb the mountains and get their good tidings," naturalist John Muir wrote. Soft blue-green peaks or rocky red edges each give important clues about the age of a mountain range. The verdant round-topped Appalachian range in eastern North America is older than the much taller Rocky Mountains to the west.

WEARING OUT

Time, weather, and erosion wear down mountain peaks. In the Appalachian Mountains, roots have established themselves over millions of years, creating expansive trees, flowers, and diverse habitat for animals. At higher elevations, the craggier Rocky Mountains contain less vegetation.

A series of continental plate collisions began forming the Appalachian range some 480 million years ago. Today sandstone ridges, deep ravines, and limestone valleys run through its forested slopes.

Mountains can also affect weather patterns, acting as natural barriers that hold moist air on the windward side of the range and keep drier conditions on the other, known as the leeward side.

The younger, rocky peaks in the Teton range contrast with the green peaks of the Appalachian Mountains (opposite).

Yes, of course I can fly that high!

MOUNTAINS RISING

Wind, water, and ice weather Earth's surface. Dynamic forces above- and belowground shape land formations and sculpt mountain ranges. The actions of tectonic plates and the process of erosion, a gradual wearing away by natural forces, form the features of most landscapes.

COLLISION COURSE

Mountains arise when continental plates collide. As plates crash into each other, their edges push up, breaking and folding into mountain ranges. These collisions lead to the formation of fold mountains, the most common type of mountain, which are created when rocks and debris from the plates are compressed into rocky outcrops.

Fold mountains are found around the world from the Appalachians in North America to the Himalaya in Asia and the Alps in Europe. All of these mountain ranges began forming after collisions many millions of years ago.

The Himalayan range is home to Mount Everest, which, at 29,035 feet (8,850 m), boasts the highest elevation of any mountain in the world. The range began forming when the Indian subcontinent collided with Eurasia about 40 to 50 million years ago. Today, as India continues its move northward, the Himalaya actively grow almost half an inch (1 cm) a year.

I'm the king of the world!

The tallest mountain range in the world, the Himalaya continue to grow today. Opposite: A computer model illustrates the geological formation underlying the range, with mountain peaks shown in white.

GO WITH THE FLOW

Rivers of ice, glaciers form on mountainsides and in polar regions. Glaciers are large masses of ice moving over land. Over time, when more snow collects than melts, it gradually compresses into a huge mass of solid ice, forming a glacier. For people living in dry regions near mountains, glacial meltwater is an important natural resource.

HEAVYWEIGHTS

The two main types of glaciers are alpine and continental. Alpine glaciers (also called valley glaciers) form in mountainous terrain. Pulled by the force of gravity, they flow downhill. Over time they carve valleys in mountain ranges, such as Switzerland's Gorner Glacier did. As glaciers creep downward, with the powerful force of their own weight and pressure, they topple huge rocks and move massive boulders. Large landmasses covered in ice are called continental ice sheets. Unconstrained by valleys and mountains, these glaciers can spread out in all directions, blanketing valleys, plains, and mountains, and covering enormous areas of land. Antarctica and Greenland both contain massive ice sheets. During the last ice age more than 10,000 years ago, ice sheets covered much of North America. As heavy glaciers melted, land adjusted in a long overdue reaction called postglacial rebound. In areas like the Great Lakes and the Gulf of Bothnia, near Finland, land continues to rise.

In Resurrection Bay, Alaska, a kayaker navigates an ice cave. Opposite: An icebreaker carves a trail through the Baltic Sea's Gulf of Bothnia for incoming boats.

THE TOP OF THE WORLD

EXPLORE THE TALLEST PEAKS OF AFRICA, ASIA, AND NORTH AMERICA.

MOUNT KILIMANJARO

Africa's highest mountain, Mount Kilimanjaro stands 19,340 feet (5,895 m) high in Tanzania. Rising amid coastal scrubland, its snowcapped peak is considered one of the world's most accessible high summits. The dormant volcano rises over the surrounding savanna, montane forest, and alpine desert. Elephants, leopards, antelope, and other wildlife roam nearby.

The snowy, sheer peaks of Mount Everest rise up in the Himalaya.

DENALI

At 20,310 feet high (6,190 m), Denali is the tallest peak in North America. Alaska's Athabaskan people have traditionally called the mountain Denali, meaning "the high one," in their native language. Named Mount McKinley, after U.S. president William McKinley, in 1917, it was officially renamed Denali in 2015. The mountain rises in Alaska's Denali National Park, surrounded by more than six million acres (2.4 million hectares) of taiga forest and alpine tundra.

Wonder if Mighty Eagle's up there . . .

MOUNT EVEREST

The highest mountain in the world, Mount Everest rises 29,035 feet (8,850 m) in the Himalayan range, straddling China and Nepal. The first successful summit of the mountain was in 1953, when New Zealander Edmund Hillary and Sherpa Tenzing Norgay reached its peak. "It's not the mountain we conquer," Hillary wrote, "but ourselves." Life at the top of the world can be dangerous. Recent avalanches in 2014 and 2015 tragically took the lives of expedition workers and climbers.

BOMB

TALL, DARK, AND . . . EXPLOSIVE

Bomb is steady and self-assured—most of the time. But when he gets surprised or stressed, things blow up quickly. He's like a stick of dynamite, operating with a long fuse, but watch out—when it goes off, *kaboom!* He detonates everything in sight.

Well-liked by the rest of the flock, Bomb's good-hearted nature lets others overlook his explosive episodes. He strives for order and calm, and he remains cautious around outsiders. He practices the quiet hobby of writing calligraphy. Unlike Chuck, Bomb doesn't feel the need to impress anyone, except maybe to spark his instructor Matilda's interest during class.

TAKE A HIKE

When facing a challenge, it's natural to want to go outside to clear your head. A breath of fresh air brings new perspectives. Just as Red journeys up a mountain seeking help, many people find the act of hiking invigorating and healing, like nature's remedy to life's tests. Whether walking around the block or scaling a mountain peak, it starts with the basics: Put one foot in front of the other. Feel the mental clarity and creativity ignite.

Nobody tells me to take a hike!

WILD AND FREE

Some hikers like an invigorating day hike, others prefer a grueling trek. Every year an estimated two to three million visitors hike portions of the scenic 2,189-mile (3,523 km) Appalachian Trail, which runs along a mountain chain from Maine to Georgia in the United States. Yet only a small percentage of those adventurous hikers attempt the entire trail, and in most years less than 30 percent of those attempts are successful. Since 1936 only about 15,000 hike completions have been recorded.

Across the country, the 2,650-mile (4,265 km) Pacific Crest Trail runs parallel to the United States' western coast. Hiking the trail solo was a life-changing experience for author Cheryl Strayed, who chronicled it in her book *Wild.* "It had only to do with how it felt to be in the wild," Strayed wrote. "With what it was like to walk for miles for no reason other than to witness the accumulation of trees and meadows, mountains and deserts, streams and rocks, rivers and grasses, sunrises and sunsets."

A rock climber grabs on to the edge of a rock face on Baffin Island, Canada. Opposite: A hiker absorbs the expansive view in Alaska's Denali National Park.

GONE CAMPING

For centuries, people gathered around the campfire under the stars and traded stories. Over the past 100 years, camping itself has grown into a popular recreational activity. Today kids and adults enjoy roasting marshmallows for s'mores over open, crackling fires and telling ghost stories.

LIGHT MY FIRE

Camping in the United States took off in the 1960s, when motor vehicle travel increased and camping supplies improved in quality and price. People began traveling farther away from their homes, to national and state parks all over the country. They could pitch a tent and stay at their scenic destination, and a camping culture was born.

"The fire is the main comfort of the camp," naturalist Henry David Thoreau wrote. Different styles of campfires serve different purposes: Fast-burning tepee fires produce high heat and light; longer-lasting log cabin fires (stacked as in a log home) emit less warmth and light.

Campers enjoy other outdoor activities, such as hiking, boating, fishing, hunting, and climbing. Outdoor trips bring memorable experiences, like the surprises Red, Chuck, and Bomb face during their adventure up the mountain.

Fire brings warmth, light, and the heat needed to cook food at campsites, including a remote one in Patagonia (opposite).

TYING THE KNOT

IN A SURVIVAL SITUATION, A TWIST OF A KNOT CAN HAVE A BIG IMPACT.

SQUARE KNOT

The square knot (also called the reef knot) ties two objects together or joins two separate ropes. It's one of the first knots learned by children in scouting. You take the right end of the rope under the left, cross it, and then take the left end under the right. It creates two loops that form a square shape and can slide back and forth. Since the knot lies flat, it's useful for tying bandages, packages, shoestrings, and even bundles of firewood.

The square knot, named for its shape, binds two objects together.

BOWLINE

The so-called king of knots, the bowline is a quick and easy tie often used in rescue. It creates a secure nonslip loop at the end of a line that won't tighten or expand. Bowlines can tie, bind, fasten, and secure almost anything. They can be used to pull a person out of the water or anchor something to a post. Mountain climbers often rely on bowlines during their climbs.

SHEET BEND

Rope too short? The simple and strong sheet bend is a hiker favorite. This handy knot solves the problem by joining ropes of different sizes and lengths together. It's named for its use on boats: Sailors used sheet bend knots to tie down sails, also called sheets.

A climber faces a sheer rock wall in Canyonlands National Park, Utah.

Stay **dry** while hiking. To **avoid** perspiration, layer your clothing and **peel off** or **add layers** as needed.

The **log size** that gives off the most **light** and **heat** when **burning** is roughly the thickness of a **human wrist.**

If you get caught in an **avalanche,** stick one **arm up** and **curve** the other **around** your **face** to **create** a pocket of **air.**

WILD SURVIVAL

If you find yourself in a life-or-death situation, the first rule is not to panic. Maintain a positive attitude and think your way through it. Survival priorities in the wild are based on your body's immediate needs. The majority of deaths in survival situations occur not from a lack of food or water, but from exposure to weather elements. Stay put, conserve your energy, and, if someone knows your general location, await rescue.

KEEP CALM AND CARRY ON

Build a good shelter to keep wind, rain, and snow off of you. It can be a simple debris hut, which looks like a nest for humans, made from sticks, twigs, and soil, or a dugout trench that takes advantage of snow's natural insulation. Always multitask: As you gather tinder, kindling, and wood for a fire, look out for food and a source of water.

Your actions and gear should have multiple purposes, too. "Two is one, and one is none" is a common phrase used in the military that echoes this survival principle. A space blanket can be used for emergency shelter, or to melt snow for drinking water. A Boy Scout neckerchief or a bandanna can double as an arm sling or cover from the sun. Fires provide warmth, boil drinking water, drive away insects, and can even signal your location to rescuers.

Building a shelter out of debris helps keep the elements away.

PACKING THE ESSENTIALS

BEFORE HEADING OUT ON A LONG JOURNEY, IT'S IMPORTANT TO HAVE THE ESSENTIALS IN PLACE.

FIRST-AID KIT

Disaster is a part of life. Thrilling adventures also can lead to injuries, weather-related or otherwise, which may require medical treatment. The right preparation and quick reaction time are critical in an emergency. Having a first-aid kit on hand helps outdoor adventures go more smoothly. From bandages and antibiotic ointment to foot-care products and pain-killers, a well-stocked first-aid kit helps adventurers return home safely.

TENT

A tent is a critical first line of defense against wind. By stopping airflow, it creates a more stable temperature inside. Insulated sleeping bags and layered clothing enhance warmth. At high-altitude base camps, teams use specialized tents with highly supportive tent poles that provide a strong wall structure against powerful winds. For a milder, summertime family camping trip, a basic tent will work, keeping bugs away and protecting campers from rain and morning dew. Some tents even have creature comforts like a mini-porch overhang to keep boots and gear dry outside.

How could I forget my tent?

BACKPACKER'S CHECKLIST

Shelter, water, and food are essential for any successful journey. For backpackers, a checklist of gear is also vital. Key equipment includes a compass for navigation, trail-worthy boots, trekking poles to soften impact, and a handy knife and rope. You might use carabiners to hold your keys, but they can act as pulleys for climbing and rappelling, too.

Early morning sun lights up a campsite in the Himalaya.

MIGHTY EAGLE
LEGENDARY AND MYSTERIOUS

Mighty Eagle is the most famous and mysterious Angry Bird of them all. Lofty legend surrounds this bird of prey, who's been honored with a statue in the middle of Bird Court. Birds on the island celebrate Mighty Eagle in both story and song, much like the bald eagle in the United States of America. Even Red respects Mighty Eagle after hearing stories of his heroic deeds and past adventures.

Yet for all his fame, Mighty Eagle is rarely seen by any of the birds. His majestic wings give him a unique power among the island's bird community: He alone has the power to fly. It's thought that he lives at the top of the island's highest mountain peak in a nearby cave, where he feasts on sardines.

When Red, Chuck, and Bomb realize they need help, they believe Mighty Eagle can show them the way. But first, they'll have to figure out how to reach his mountain home. Will the wisdom of Mighty Eagle guide them?

FIERCE FIGHTERS

Birds of prey are known for their speed, power, and ferocity. With aerodynamic feathers that rip through the air and formidable hunting skills, these powerful fliers shock and stun their victims. Eagles, hawks, falcons, vultures, and owls are all birds of prey. On the menu are other birds, fish, small mammals, snakes, and insects. Some vultures relish leftovers, feasting on carrion. Bald eagles are kleptoparasites, meaning they will steal another predator's kill.

LIFE ON THE WING

Birds of prey have a need for speed. Diving at more than 200 miles an hour (320 km/h), the peregrine falcon is the fastest animal on Earth. Its rigid, pointed feathers and long, narrow tail allow it to turn and shoot itself in the direction of dinner.

While food sustains birds of prey, nests provide essential shelter for their survival. Eagles and falcons reuse their sturdy stick nests over multiple years. Owls search for tree hollows or bed down in an abandoned stick nest. Most owls hunt at night and roost during the day. They detect prey with their excellent binocular vision and superb hearing.

Though pesticides once put their populations at risk, birds of prey, including bald eagles and peregrine falcons, have since rebounded across North America.

I'm the leader of this fierce flock!

114

A bald eagle snatches a fish in the Aleutian Islands, Alaska. Opposite: A peregrine falcon nose-dives.

THROUGH AN EAGLE'S EYE

EAGLES ARE REAL-LIFE ANGRY BIRDS, SOME OF THE MOST INTIMIDATING PREDATORS AROUND.

GOLDEN EAGLE

Prized for falconry, the golden eagle is a fierce hunter that power-dives for its prey. A patch of golden feathers forms a crown on the back of its head. Mammals, birds, reptiles, and insects are all dinner options for this unpicky eater. In North America, golden eagles favor portions of the western United States and Canada, where they fly and hunt over open country.

LITTLE EAGLE

A small and stocky bird of prey, the little eagle is native to Australia. The mostly terrestrial bird sports a rust-colored head, caramel-hued body, and feathered legs. It flies in tight circles, hunting rabbits and insects. Stable populations of little eagles range across the country in open forest, woodland, and savanna.

A bald eagle flashes its impressive wingspan in British Columbia, Canada.

BALD EAGLE

Perhaps no bird is more recognizable than the bald eagle, soaring with wide, powerful wings. With its pure white head and tail, yellow beak, and dark brown overcoat, the bald eagle appears in a regal fashion. Primarily a fish-eater, this water-loving bird follows coastlines and open water. Known for its aggressiveness, the bald eagle also enjoys stealing kills from other birds.

117

LIVING THE HIGH LIFE

Life in extreme mountain environments calls for extreme adaptations. As anyone who has ever stood on top of a mountain knows, it's a *long* way down. Sure-footed maneuvers at high elevations are crucial, as are staying warm and eating what's available.

ROCKY MOUNTAIN HIGH

Mountain goats, a relative to goats but actually closer to a goat-antelope, are the Olympic climbers of the mountain world. At home on North America's rocky slopes and steep cliffs, mountain goats expertly balance with their two-toed cloven hooves, which spread wide to enhance their balance. Their feet act as climbing shoes, with rough pads on the bottom to grip steep terrain. A thick, snowy coat and beard keeps mountain goats warm and camouflaged. Skilled jumpers, they can leap 12 feet (4 m) in a single bound.

Another alpine animal with a hop in its step is the Tibetan ground tit, a terrestrial bird that bounces among rocks and jumps out of the way of predators. Also called the Tibetan ground jay and Hume's groundpecker, it thrives in the alpine steppe of the Tibetan Plateau. Using its long curved bill, it pokes for prey beneath rocky crevices or digs through yak dung for insects.

In Montana's Glacier National Park, a mountain goat goes out on a limb for a lick of salt. Opposite: The Tibetan ground tit uses its curved beak to find food.

LEGENDS ON THE MOUNTAIN

GET TO KNOW A FEW OF THE ANIMALS LIVING THE HIGH LIFE.

A remote camera captures an image of the rarely seen snow leopard in India.

SNOW LEOPARDS

Known as the ghost of the mountain, the snow leopard is a solitary and elusive creature. With a dense fur coat colored white, yellow, gray, and black, it seemingly disappears into the mountains of Central Asia. Extra-large paws suit its cold surroundings, serving as snowshoes that prevent the cat from sinking into snow. A thick, long tail helps the snow leopard balance among steep and rocky cliffs, and strong chest muscles allow it to leap after ibex and sheep. Fewer than 7,000 of this endangered species remain in the wild.

Here kitty, nice kitty!

MOUNTAIN GORILLAS

The mountain gorilla lives along the volcanic green slopes of central Africa. A dominant male alpha leader, known for its signature silverback fur, leads each troop of up to 30 individuals. They nest in leaves and eat fruit, roots, and tree bark. These omnivores can weigh more than 450 pounds (200 kg). Yet habitat loss, poaching, and human unrest threaten the endangered species and the forests it inhabits in the Virunga Mountains.

PIKAS

The tiny, teddy bear–faced pika is good at hiding out in the alpine cold. From mountains in the western United States to peaks in China's northwest, the pika is one of the world's highest-dwelling animals. Comfortable in even the coldest regions, the pika is a relative of rabbits and hares. It collects and eats flowers and grasses, forming hay nests under rocky mountain crevices. It stores dried grasses to nibble on over the long winter. Pikas make a squeaky warning call to advertise predatory hawks overhead.

LEVEL 4 | *BEYOND THE ISLAND*

Discover what lies outside familiar shores

The pigs make a big impact when they arrive on Bird Island, especially on Red's home!

A *SINISTER* PLOT

Back at sea level on Bird Island, the relationship between the birds and the pigs continues to evolve. Leonard and his crew showcase their wobbly piggy creations made with slingshots and TNT boxes. Although the inventions are precarious, and potentially explosive, the birds don't think about the chance that their new friends, the pigs, might be up to something sneaky.

EGGS-PLOSIVE RELATIONSHIPS

Leonard flings grapes at the birds with his slingshot to distract them, and a couple birds eagerly gobble up the fruit. Meanwhile the other pigs place boxes of dynamite around Bird Village, stacking them next to buildings, tents, and trees. It seems that these new visitors aren't just here to bring presents after all.

A HEROIC RETURN

After a devastating visit with Mighty Eagle, Red, Chuck, and Bomb come back down the mountain. They are shocked to see explosives littering their village. And their treasured eggs are nowhere to be found! Chuck rushes to warn the rest of the birds, but they're too busy celebrating with the pigs at a laser light show to bother listening.

TIME TO GET ANGRY!

Red and Bomb hurry over to the pigs' ship
to see if they can find the missing eggs.
The two of them try, unsuccessfully, to
use the pigs' trampoline to rescue the eggs
from the ship. With disaster looming, Red
finally realizes he must take on the role of
a real leader. He's determined to retrieve
the community's precious eggs, but he
knows it's going to take a group effort.
There's no more time for calm and happy,
Red says heatedly to the other birds. It's
time to get angry!

The pigs quickly swing into action and show the birds a new contraption they haven't seen before—the slingshot.

X MARKS THE SPOT

Maps help us understand our relationship to the world and to each other. The human desire to identify, measure, record, and analyze information drives mapmaking, also called cartography, and brings new meaning to land, sea, and sky. From ancient Babylonian maps, made in the sixth century B.C., to the Greeks' classic scientific investigations into the universe, maps have been made, studied, and improved upon over generations and across cultures.

VOYAGES ACROSS THE WORLD

Thousands of years ago, early Polynesian seafarers in the Pacific Ocean ventured for long distances between islands in voyaging canoes, without the aid of navigational tools. Relying on oral traditional knowledge and natural signs, such as tides, currents, and the positions of stars, they kept track of patterns with stick charts made out of reeds and shells.

With increasing European exploration in the late 15th and 16th centuries, ship charts and navigational instruments—like compasses and sextants, which calculate latitude and longitude against the angle of the horizon—pushed the frontiers of exploration even farther. In 1585, Flemish cartographer Gerardus Mercator created a groundbreaking map with a grid of lines and angles, helping voyagers plot courses as they sailed. Today, with new place-names and shifting borders, maps continue to change and improve.

Now, how do I get to Bird Island from here?

A tapestry reveals an early map of Spain. Opposite: Sextants, such as this bronze one, helped explorers chart new waters.

MAP PIONEERS

The United States nearly doubled in size in 1803 after President Thomas Jefferson secured the Louisiana Purchase. Yet without reliable maps west of the Appalachian Mountains, the area remained a mystery to non-Native Americans. Jefferson directed the Corps of Discovery, led by Meriwether Lewis and co-captain William Clark, to head west, asking them to find the supposed Northwest Passage for trade, and to survey and map the land as well.

AN EPIC JOURNEY

Along with their invaluable Native American guide, Sacagawea, and her husband, the team traveled nearly 8,000 miles (13,000 km) round-trip. Although they gave up on finding the Northwest Passage, they recorded a wealth of information about the route and land, along with plant and animal species. Sacagawea's wilderness expertise and communication with native tribes was indispensable, as was a surprise reunion between Sacagawea and her brother, Shoshone chief Cameahwait. The chief gave the group navigational advice and horses.

"From this place we had an extensive view of these stupendous mountains principally covered with snow," Lewis wrote in his journal. "To one unacquainted with them it would have seemed impossible ever to have escaped." In 1805, the team finally reached the Pacific Ocean. Along the way they recorded the first detailed maps of the West, spurring westward expansion.

A painting shows Meriwether Lewis and William Clark by the Columbia River, with Sacagawea and her family. Opposite: The explorers' journals chronicle their adventures.

NEXT-GENERATION MAPMAKING

I'm helping!

It's easier than ever to find out where you're going. Rapid changes in technology have created new frontiers in mapmaking and expanded the scale of possibility. In the 21st century, an unprecedented growth in information technology and geographic information systems (GIS) has transformed the way we see our planet.

A BIRD'S-EYE VIEW

Today satellite images from Global Positioning Systems (GPS) give people easy and accurate information about their location around the world. Maps that in the past might have taken months or years to make are now available in interactive form on a smartphone in an instant. Google Earth has opened up the world to virtual explorers everywhere.

Remote-sensing systems capture data from a distance, similar to the way aerial reconnaissance photography captured inaccessible areas during World War II. Radar and sonar also record surface features of land and sea.

Personalized on-the-go mapping and crowd-sourced cartography now take more people more places than ever before.

A satellite image highlights the vast watershed of Russia's Lena River, one of the world's longest. Opposite: Surveying instruments help measure distance.

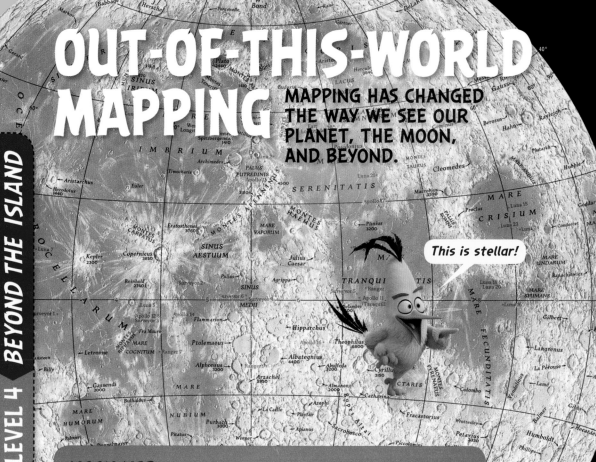

OUT-OF-THIS-WORLD MAPPING

MAPPING HAS CHANGED THE WAY WE SEE OUR PLANET, THE MOON, AND BEYOND.

This is stellar!

MOON MAP

The violent history of the moon is revealed through maps. Blasted by comets and meteors, the moon's surface is scarred with craters. In 1969, *National Geographic* published the first map to show both the near and far sides of the lunar surface on a single sheet. That same year, American astronauts first landed on the moon at the Sea of Tranquility. To this day, astronaut Neil Armstrong's steps still appear on the moon's surface since, unlike Earth, the moon lacks an atmosphere of wind or water to wash them away.

PTOLEMY'S MAP

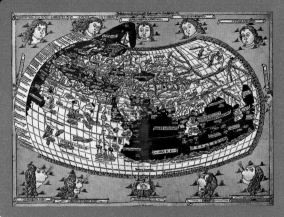

Often called the "father of geography," Claudius Ptolemy mapped land and sky in the second century A.D. His world map was part of his eight-volume *Geography*, which listed 8,000 locations, many of them in the Mediterranean region. His map had some hits and misses (among the misses, South Africa connected to Asia in the south), but he described how to design a world atlas using a system of grid coordinates.

GOOGLE EARTH

Google has transformed the way we see our planet. From its Street View neighborhood snapshots to soaring flights over metropolitan cities—including 3-D layered images of structures like the Roman Colosseum—Google Earth allows you to explore Earth straight from your device. This technological innovation in mapping is advancing learning in countless ways, from tracking the spread of wildfires to following the movements of elephants.

In 1969, National Geographic created a seminal map of the moon's surface.

TERENCE

THE STRONG AND SILENT TYPE

Like a brawny beast, Terence looks and acts intimidating, but there's more to this glowering giant than visible at first glance. Terence is the biggest of all the island birds. He doesn't say much; all anyone knows is that "an incident" led him to anger management class. As he lumbers along the village streets, he mainly communicates in growls and grunts.

Many in the community are fearful of what secret the silent behemoth may hold. Is he up to something, or is Terence just misunderstood? Terence has a surprising talent that he wants to share with the world, if they're finally ready to hear it.

NAVIGATING BY THE STARS

Before we had the Internet, video games, television, movies, or radio, people looked to the night sky, which inspired legends of myths and monsters. Sky-watching is one of the most ancient forms of entertainment and storytelling. Over the ages, mesmerized by the faraway sparkling light of celestial bodies like the moon, sun, stars, and planets, people have looked up, searching the sky for answers.

ANCIENT STARGAZERS

Mesopotamians remarked on distinct patterns dotting the sky. Ancient Egyptians predicted the flooding of the Nile River for agriculture using the position of Sirius, the brightest star. Building on these traditions, in the second century A.D., Egyptian-Greek astronomer Claudius Ptolemy codified a list of 48 constellations, or groups of stars, in his astrological handbook *Almagest*. He also mentioned the zodiac, which means circle of animals in Greek. The zodiac follows the path of the sun across the sky and divides the sky into 12 parts, or "sun symbols," that correspond to different animals and creatures, such as Pisces (a pair of fish) and Taurus (a bull). Today many people follow their horoscopes based on the zodiac sign tied to their birthday.

Adventurers and backyard enthusiasts still use the night sky for navigation and inspiration. It starts with location, such as whether you live in the Northern or Southern Hemisphere, and what season it is. Like a compass, the North Star, also called Polaris, is a handy reference point that orients people due north.

A time-lapse image displays a famous spot in the night sky, the North Star, which guides people.

STARGAZING FROM YOUR BACKYARD

Stargazing starts with curiosity and a question: What's that? You can start exploring the nighttime sky from your own backyard. It's a simple, fun, and fascinating activity. Take a walk outside on a clear night (the less artificial light, the better). With just the naked eye, you can spy the moon, stars, constellations, planets, shooting stars, and galaxies more than two million light-years away!

THE NIGHTTIME SKY

Watching the night sky is an easy family activity and hobby for all ages. Get to know star patterns and astrological charts. Find a dark location. Allow your eyes 15 to 20 minutes to get used to the dark first. Look for recognizable star patterns, like the Big Dipper. Find the Milky Way's blurry band of light. Look for Venus, which is relatively close to Earth. In the summertime, take in the Perseid meteor shower, found near the constellation Perseus. The more you practice, the more you'll find!

With a telescope or binoculars, you can see even more. Consider starting out with binoculars, which give a wider field of view straight out in front of you, making it easier to find objects. So head outside, kick back, and look up. Take in the moon's dramatic craters and mountains. The romance and beauty of the night sky is endless.

Starry skies at night take us beyond our world. Opposite: A telescope can bring the stars closer to you.

Are you a little starstruck, or is it just me?

SUPERSTARS OF THE NIGHT SKY

IN CULTURES AROUND THE WORLD, PEOPLE HAVE TOLD STORIES ABOUT THE STARS IN THE SKY.

ORION

The hunter known for his famous belt, Orion is one of the most recognizable constellations in the sky. His spot near the celestial equator illuminates him year-round. Some of the sky's brightest stars make up Orion's outline, including red-tinted Betelgeuse and supergiant Rigel, which shines about 50,000 times as bright as the sun. The fierce Orion wields a club in one hand and a lion pelt in the other.

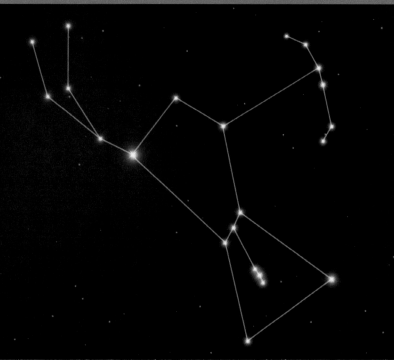

CASSIOPEIA

Reigning over the night sky, Cassiopeia the queen sits forever chained to her throne in the Milky Way. In the Greek myth, the gods banished Cassiopeia to the sky after she boasted that her daughter, Andromeda, was more beautiful than the daughters of the sea god.

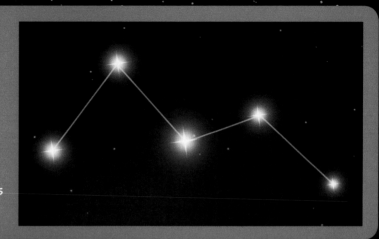

URSA MAJOR

Latin for "great bear," Ursa Major is one of the most true-to-form constellations. A main part of this famous 20-star constellation is the Big Dipper, shaped like a pot with a handle. Highlighted by cultures across the world, the ancient pattern evokes different images for different groups. Native Americans saw warriors chasing a bear in the handle of the Big Dipper, Egyptians said it was a hippopotamus. Others thought it might be a chariot, a wagon, or a team of oxen.

143

The Milky Way galaxy glows above the treetops, seen from California.

There are tens of billions of galaxies in the universe. Our Milky Way galaxy is spiral shaped.

Lewis and Clark's Native American guide, Sacagawea, brought her newborn baby on the group's famous U.S. westward journey.

A star is made up almost entirely of the gases hydrogen and helium.

ANIMAL ISLANDS

Although people have taken over much of the world, on some islands animals still take center stage. Wild horses enchant visitors at Assateague Island, a national seashore near Chincoteague, Virginia, and Ocean City, Maryland. More than 300 species of birds, including many migratory shorebirds, also stop to find food in the uninhabited barrier island's salt marshes, pine forest, and beaches. Each summer on the Virginia side, some 40,000 people gather to witness the Chincoteague Pony Swim, where about 150 wild ponies swim across the Assateague Channel.

A DOMINANT DISPLAY

On Seal Island near Cape Town, South Africa, seals steal the show. A huge colony of 64,000 Cape fur seals inhabits the five-acre (two hectare) rocky outcrop in False Bay. It's also home to many seabirds. Yet the real drama peaks when predator and prey meet. Sensing a good meal, great white sharks encircle the island at hidden depths, waiting for seals to appear. When one approaches or attempts to leave its sanctuary, a great white rockets to the surface, hurtling itself and the seal some ten feet (3 m) up out of the water before chomping down on dinner.

Life's a beach for Cape fur seals in South Africa—until the sharks arrive. Opposite: Wild horses spar on Assateague Island in Maryland and Virginia.

HOGGIN' THE ISLAND

The pigs on Bird Island aren't the only hogs stealing food. On the uninhabited island of Big Major Cay in the outer Exuma area of the Bahamas, a group of feral pigs runs the show. It's unknown exactly how they got to the island, which locals call Pig Beach. It's possible they're a holdover from a shipwreck, or they were left by sailors who intended to eat them but never returned. No matter how they wound up there, today the island is most definitely under piggy rule.

REAL-LIFE PIGGY ISLAND

Pigs beat the heat lounging under palm trees on white-sand beaches and taking afternoon dips in crystal clear waters. They survive on cast-off food from passing ships and readily accept gifts of food from tourists boating by to see them. But beware: The pigs are curious, hungry, and surprisingly strong swimmers. They'll swim out to your boat and throw a hoof over it in search of snacks.

Swimming in tropical waters and lounging on the beach (opposite) is just another day in paradise for these wild pigs.

LEONARD

SLICK-TALKING AND SHOWY

The charismatic Leonard serves as ambassador for the pigs. When he and his ship arrive on Bird Island, Leonard claims to come in peace, showering the birds with showy gifts. He and his rambunctious crew (seen below) quickly win over the trusting bird community—all except Red, who wonders if there isn't a more sinister reason for their visit.

Red can't help noticing Leonard's sneaky looks and the dark cracks behind his crooked grin, and he wonders if the pig is playing a dangerous game. Red's determined to protect his island home—and the eggs. The question is: Will he be able to convince the others before it's too late?

GOING THE DISTANCE

Migrating animals rely on instinct to spark epic journeys. With their keen sensory awareness, many birds, mammals, fish, and insects can tell when their resources, like food or daylight, are dwindling. They respond to a basic need to breed and raise young. These animals take action and embark on migrations, crossing oceans and fording predator-laden rivers to reach home territories. All this risk comes with a simple reward: survival.

AN INCREDIBLE JOURNEY

Still, leaving can be dangerous. When herds of wildebeests on Africa's Serengeti Plain migrate across crocodile-infested waters, one wrong move can separate a wildebeest from the herd, landing it inside a crocodile's powerful jaws.

When the ground starts to freeze in the fall, Canadian geese migrate south in pursuit of warmer weather—and food. These honking waterbirds aren't picky eaters. They find plenty of grasses, roots, and leaves near water and in fields. The flock travels in a V-formation, with an experienced bird at the helm, leading the way.

Chaaarge!

Wildebeests brave Africa's crocodile-infested Mara River during their migration. Opposite: Canadian geese flock together in migratory flight.

ANIMAL TRACKERS

From tracking sharks to tagging sea turtles, scientists follow animal journeys around the world. People of all ages can help, too. Citizen science volunteers participate in nature walks along the beach, looking for tags that give key identifying information about injured or deceased marine animals. If they see a stranded animal, like a sea turtle, they check its tag and contact authorities. By helping scientists gather population information, people are contributing to conservation efforts for the next generation.

ADD IT UP

Many animals are making waves, like social media celebrity Mary Lee, a great white shark with her own Twitter handle: @MaryLeeShark. Tagged by researchers in 2012 in Cape Cod, Massachusetts, the 16-foot (5 m), 3,400-pound (1,500 kg) shark zigzags along the Eastern Seaboard in the Atlantic Ocean. Her back-and-forth movements and closeness to the shore are surprising scientists.

Tagging songbirds helps scientists monitor the health of bird populations and better understand their migratory patterns. Scientists are also learning more about how birds use stars to navigate and how they follow magnetic fields.

A migrating bobolink in Nebraska is banded for tracking. Opposite: On the Galápagos Islands, a scalloped hammerhead's dorsal fin is tagged.

155

MOST EPIC MIGRATIONS

THESE INCREDIBLE ANIMALS UNDERTAKE EPIC JOURNEYS IN THE AIR, ON LAND, AND AT SEA.

MONARCH BUTTERFLIES

Monarch butterflies embark on one of the most colorful and remarkable journeys of any insect. Millions of the brightly colored black, orange, and white butterflies migrate thousands of miles across North America to California and Mexico each winter. Only the last generation of monarchs born each year undergoes the migration, departing for warmer weather in late summer or fall. In spring they resume their flight back to the north or east. Despite making the round-trip journey only once, monarchs somehow intrinsically know where to go—some even find the same oyamel fir trees used by previous generations!

LEATHERBACK SEA TURTLES

The biggest sea turtle species on Earth, leatherbacks have been exploring the sea since the time of the dinosaurs. Deep-diving travelers, they move through every ocean except the Arctic and waters around Antarctica. The massive reptiles weigh up to 2,000 pounds (900 kg) each and may swim more than 1,000 miles (1,600 km) to reach their nesting beaches in tropical waters. Shortly after laying its eggs, a female heads back out to sea. Leatherback populations are stable in the North Atlantic but are declining in the Pacific, where they often fall prey to fishermens' nets.

ARCTIC TERNS

Flying up to 55,000 miles (88,500 km) round-trip, the arctic tern leads the flock as a long-distance champion. With its signature snappy, quick flight, forked tail, and long tail streamers, the black-capped, red-billed bird migrates incredible distances each year. In late summer or early autumn, the tern embarks on a trip that takes 90 days each way. From its nesting home in the Arctic, the tern crosses the oceans in the Northern Hemisphere, then dips south, ultimately reaching subantarctic waters rich in pack ice and food.

I thought we were sharing!

Arctic terns make the longest migration of any bird in the world.

ACKNOWLEDGMENTS

We would like to extend our thanks to the terrific people who worked hard to make this project come together so quickly and so well.

ROVIO

Rollo de Walden, Ilona Lindh, Terhi Haikonen, and Aino Greis

NATIONAL GEOGRAPHIC

Michelle Cassidy, Bridget E. Hamilton, Nicole Lazarus, Kristin Sladen, Jonathan Halling, Lisa A. Walker, Katie Olsen, Nicole Miller, Mike O'Connor, and Marshall Kiker

We'd like to thank Geoffrey S. LeBaron from the National Audubon Society and Terry Engelder of Pennsylvania State University for their help and expertise.

I'd like to thank everyone in my flock, especially my mom and dad, husband, and children, for their inspiration and support. —CUB

ABOUT THE AUTHOR

Christy Ullrich Barcus is an editor at *National Geographic* magazine and editor of National Geographic's Polar Bear Watch blog. Her writing focuses on natural history, culture, and science topics and appears regularly on National Geographic's website. She lives in Virginia with her husband and their two children.

ILLUSTRATIONS CREDITS